THE
MILLENNIUM
CLOTHING

A Pictorial History of the Past One Thousand Years

Sue Hamilton

ABDO
& Daughters

Visit us at
www.abdopub.com

Published by ABDO Publishing Company, 4940 Viking Drive, Edina, MN 55435.
Copyright ©2000 by Abdo Consulting Group, Inc. International copyrights
reserved in all countries. No part of this book may be reproduced in any form without written
permission from the publisher.

Printed in the United States.

Art Direction: John Hamilton

Cover photos: Corbis, AP/Wideworld Photos
Interior photos: Corbis, AP/Wideworld Photos

Library of Congress Cataloging–in–Publication Data

Hamilton, Sue L., 1959-
    Clothing / Sue Hamilton.
        p. cm. -- (The millennium)
    Summary: A pictorial survey of the way people around the world have dressed over the
past 1000 years.
    ISBN 1-57765-358-0
    1. Costume--Juvenile literature. 2. Clothing and dress--Juvenile literature. [1. Clothing
and dress--History.] I. Title. II. Millennium (Minneapolis, Minn.)

GT518 .H35 2000
391--dc21

99-043240

CONTENTS

INTRODUCTION

Fashion has developed throughout history to show who a person really is.

Why do we have clothes? It's easy to answer that question when it's zero degrees. Unless our skin is covered to keep in our body heat, it wouldn't take long before we'd freeze. Some desert nomads wear many layers of clothing. Other tribes wear minimal coverings. Yet everyone wears some type of clothing. Why? To cover up parts of our bodies we want to keep private, and to cover up what we don't want sunburned. However, if clothing is used only to protect our bodies from cold, heat, or prying eyes, why has clothing changed so much in the last thousand years? One word: style. Fashions have developed to show who a person really is.

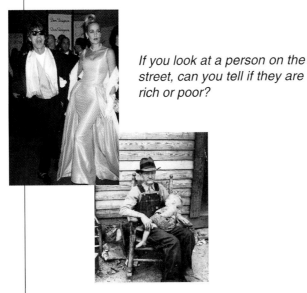

If you look at a person on the street, can you tell if they are rich or poor?

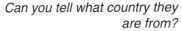

Can you tell what country they are from?

Simply based on how a person dresses, can you guess his or her age?

Can you guess a person's religious beliefs based on how they dress?

What clothes are worn, how they are worn, who designed them, the colors used, and what they are made of all help indicate a person's position in life—now and hundreds of years ago.

Let's take a look at clothing through the ages. Pay attention to the styles. Even though fashions have changed dramatically from era to era, people's desire to be "in fashion" has never changed.

BEFORE THE MILLENNIUM

In early cultures, a great deal of time was spent finding basic necessities, like food and shelter. However, even the earliest people adorned themselves with skins and jewelry fashioned from the animals they hunted. As time passed and people went from hunting and fishing cultures to farming, a whole new opportunity for "fashion" opened up.

Early people believed that by wearing a fierce animal's skin, one took on that animal's spirit.

Animal Skins

Stone Age people discovered ways to fit animal skins more securely to their bodies. Animal bones or tusks were fashioned into needles. Knives were used to punch holes in the hide. Thread was made from animal tendons. In addition, early people created necklaces made of animal teeth or bones—proving the hunter's strength and honor.

Soaking and pounding tree bark into a soft cloth known as tapa created some of the earliest known fashions.

Plant Fibers

As cultures evolved from hunting and fishing to farming, people soon realized that plant fibers (cotton, linen, and hemp), animal fleece (wool), and even the filament from a caterpillar (silk) could be woven into fabrics. From that point, clothing changed from functional into fashionable.

In the hot climate of Egypt, clothing was considered an ornament. Egyptians developed a very light, transparent linen cloth. Men and women wore loincloths over which was draped either a skirt (for men) or a simple dress.

In Egypt, a peplos was a large rectangular piece of wool or linen, draped over the body and fastened with pins. Small, oval weights were sometimes sewn into the hem of a peplos to keep the material closer to the body. The pinless chiton (right) eventually replaced the peplos.

Tanning Leather

The process of tanning leather—rubbing it with oil, alum, and vegetable substances—produced a soft fabric out of animal hides. This leather was made into clothing, as well as bags for carrying water, grain, or objects. Most popular, however, were shoes. The leather was colored and decorated with jewels and embroidery. In Babylonia, their dyed red shoes (caligas) were sought after even by Roman emperors.

The draped fashion in early Greece was known as a chiton. In Rome, it was the tunica. A longer version was known as the toga. Although the toga was usually white and worn for special occasions, the everyday fashions were often dyed and/or embroidered.

INCAS, MAYAS, AND AZTECS

The Incas embroidered or wove geometric shapes and stylized images of animals and humans into their clothes.

The Inca, Maya, and Aztec were great civilizations. Living in the Andean Mountains, the Incas wove fabric from the wool of alpacas, llamas, and vicuñas. Down on the hot plains of Mesoamerica, the Mayas and Aztecs wore cotton, maguey cactus cloth, and yucca and palm fiber cloth. The more finely made and beautifully decorated the cloth, the greater one's status. Yet all clothing was simple—often a single piece of material draped over or around a part of the body.

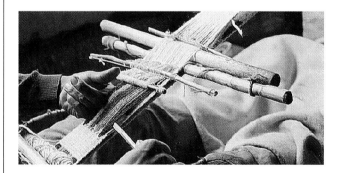

Still widely used today, the back-strap loom was used by weavers throughout South America and Mesoamerica.

Inca

The poncho slipped over the head and was sewn at the sides. It was both a cloak and a blanket. Ponchos were such important garments that the dead were buried with them. People wore knitted wool or cotton caps.

Feather shirts and headdresses of the Inca people were created by carefully stitching each feather to a piece of cotton cloth. Tropical birds were hunted and raised in captivity for their beautiful feathers.

Maya

A Mayan woman wore a huipil—a straight dress sewn up the sides with holes left for the neck and arms. Mayas never cut their cloth—they wove it to the exact size needed. Hair ribbons were made of a woven cloth 80 feet (24 m) long. Their red dye came from the cochineal bug. Mollusks provided purple dye.

Aztec

The length, colors, and decorations of Aztec clothing were determined by one's status. If people disobeyed the strict clothing rules, they were killed. Aztec men wore a simple loincloth and a cloak made from a square of material, knotted on the right shoulder. Women wore ankle-length skirts and sleeveless tunics. Ear, nose, and lip plugs were made of shells, polished stones, or gold and silver.

Feathered headdresses were worn on special occasions. The green feathers of the quetzal bird were most valued because the bird was linked with the Aztec god Quetzalcoatl, the god of knowledge and creation. Headbands held their hair in position. Only nobles or warriors wore headbands decorated with gold or precious jewels.

The best warriors wore jaguar and eagle suits (left). These were padded and starched, but were no match for the weaponry of the Spanish soldiers. Wooden shields (below) were padded and decorated with feathers.

Maasai women wear beaded necklaces, which show if they are married, whether they have children, and how wealthy they are.

AFRICA

Africa is a land of forests, but also of deserts, savannas, and high mountain ranges. Over 1,000 languages are spoken there. People's culture and lifestyles vary greatly. The San of the Kalahari wear very little, while the men of Algeria wear several layers of loose clothing. Both live in a desert region, but their appearances are vastly different. Such is the case with many different people and tribes on this huge continent.

The Zulus, led by King Shaka, fought for their lands in the 1800s. Their elaborate headdresses of ostrich feathers and beautifully painted shields distinguished them.

Kuba

The Kuba people of Zaire weave cut-pile cloth. The base cloth is a piece of woven raffia, which is a grasslike fiber of the raffia palm. It is used to make a wide variety of everyday things such as robes.

In many parts of western Africa, a married woman wears a large and elaborate head-tie, usually of the same material as her dress. The head-tie is a single piece of fabric that she folds and wraps according to her social status. Usually, the greater the height and size of the headdress, the more important she is.

Ndebele

Members of the Ndebele tribe of South Africa lengthen their necks by wrapping them with brass and copper rings called *iindzila*. The rings are first worn at marriage. More are added over time until a woman's head may perch a foot above her shoulders. The bands press downward, deforming the collarbone. Today, Ndebele women are shedding their traditional ornaments, although they may sometimes wear a set of removable plastic rings.

In Madagascar, cotton, silk, and raffia are woven into colorful shawls (right) that are worn by men and women. The designs are so complicated that the weaver sometimes uses bits of numbered paper to figure out at which point the pattern is to be formed.

Copper wire jewelry (above) is found in many parts of eastern and southern Africa. Bracelets, armlets, and anklets are usually worn by women and can weigh up to 30 pounds (14 kg).

Algeria

Men of Algeria wear loose, baggy trousers and long cotton tops to keep cool. A piece of cloth, or veil (left), is wrapped around the head with a narrow gap for the eyes. This protects the wearer from sun, heat, and windblown sand.

In North Africa, a Mohammedan sheik wears an aba—which serves as a coat, overcoat, raincoat, or blanket. Usually it is white or black cloth with a wide border, probably red with a single yellow stripe. Underneath is a tobe—a white cotton shirt reaching to the ankles. A turban is worn on the head.

THE MIDDLE EAST

Under the laws of Islam, women are required to cover their entire bodies when in public.

A s one of the earliest civilizations (beginning over 5,000 years ago), Egypt's fashions reflected the warmth of the climate. The earliest Egyptians, if they wore anything, wrapped themselves in a white linen loincloth (a schenti) or a tight-fitting skirt called a kalasiris. Romans conquered Egypt in 30 B.C., and Moslems came in A.D. 640. Today, Egypt is made up mostly of Moslems. Moslem people follow the teaching of the prophet Muhammad. Their fashion is dictated by the laws of the Koran, the holy book of Islam. Some follow the rules; others interpret these fashion codes less strictly.

The ancient Egyptian woman (left figurine) is wearing a kalasiris, a basic garment for over 2,000 years. It hugged the body from bust to ankle, held up by straps or a wide collar. The quality of the kalasiris' fabric showed the social class of the wearer.

Tarboosh, or fez, is the Arabic name of the brimless dark red or black felt cap, which has its origin in ancient Greece. Both men and women wear it.

The haik, or burka, is a long piece of cotton or woolen cloth, which envelops the Algerian woman in public. It is draped over the tarboosh and the body, belted at the waist, covering the chalwar and pantaloons.

Kaffiyeh

Kaffiyeh is a headdress of cotton, linen, or silk. It can be plain or striped and varied in name, pattern, and color. Worn for thousands of years, it remains the favorite head covering of the Arab for all occasions. It is even worn with Western dress. Folded into a triangle and placed upon the head, two points fall over the shoulders providing a tie, if wanted, and one hangs in back to protect the neck. A skullcap is often worn underneath. The agal is the hoop or fillet of thick cords of wool or goat's hair that holds the kaffiyeh in place. The agal is often wound around with gold and silver threads.

The kibr, also called a gallibiya or caftan (left and right), is the traditional robe of the Arab-speaking world. Camel herders, called tuareg, wear a turban as protection against sand and sun. A noble's litham is black or blue, while commoners wear a white one.

The huke (left) is a square of woolen cloth large enough to envelop the whole figure.

For men, the traditional pantaloons are very full and draped and reach to the knee or ankle. A gandoura is a white or colored shirt, long-sleeved or sleeveless, of cotton or wool. The short Spanish jacket, or bolero, reaches to the waistline and is ornamented with braid. It is worn open over a fine white shirt and a widecrushed-silk sash of brilliant color.

INDIA & AFFGHANISTAN

A sari is a common garment among Hindu women in India.

The richness of the Indus River Valley drew people together. They created some of the world's first cities some 5,000 years ago and formed India. The great religions of Hinduism and Buddhism were developed there, influencing their fashions. Full, white cotton fashions are worn by men and women, which keep them cool in the hot desert temperatures.

Sari

A sari is the most important garment of a Hindu female from 13 or 14 years of age. It is a cotton or silk piece of fabric six yards (5 m) long. Some are woven with gold and silver threads. Wealthy women may own a hundred or more. If they ever need to sell one, a dealer weighs it for metal content and pays the appropriate price. When a Moslem woman wears a Hindu sari, it is never made of pure silk because the Koran forbids the wearing of pure silk.

The choli is the short shirt or blouse worn under the sari.

Moslem women wear a chadar, which they hold together up to their eyes, thus being completely covered while in public.

Nehru Tunic

A nehru tunic, or choga (left), is worn principally in Kashmir and Punjab. It is knee-length, with side slits, a standing collar, and buttons down the center front. Under it are worn white linen trousers in jodhpur fashion.

The turban (right and below) is a piece of white or colorful silk or cotton measuring 5 to 25 yards (4.5 to 23 m) in length. It is wound round the head in various ways, with the end left hanging or knotted on the left side. The turban's tail goes over the shoulder and may be used as a dust veil, purse, handkerchief, or more.

The full white cotton pantaloons (right) and tunic are worn by farmers. The tunic skirt is held up by the cloth tied around the waist.

Kurta Shirts

The Sikh of Ludhiana wear kurta shirts and distinctive turbans (below). Moroccan leather slippers (left) with pointed-toed shoes are considered fashionable.

CHINA & JAPAN

China is the most populated country in the world. It is very diverse. People from different parts of the country can dress quite differently. China's written history stretches back 3,500 years—longer than any other nation. They discovered the secrets of the silkworm, using the threads it spins in its cocoon to create the beautiful material silk.

A kimono is a loose gown tied with a sash. It remains Japan's national costume, despite the fact that Western dress is now more commonly worn.

Japan may have once been connected to the Asian mainland, but once it became an island, it developed its own culture. Powerful families and their samurai (right) ruled. It was a military culture, but also one that centered on their religion: Zen Buddhism.

Japan

The masculine kimono is dark in color and has shorter sleeves, but otherwise is similar to the feminine robe. All garments of men and women fasten from left to right. The man's robe is ankle-length and his family crest is embroidered or stenciled on each side of the chest, in center back, and at the top of the sleeves. For daily wear, a wide sash called the heko-obi goes around the waist two or three times and ties in a loose bow. The kaku-obi, a sash of heavy silk, is worn on formal occasions and is tied in back in a double knot. The feminine kimono may be floor-length or shorter, the longer being held by a cord tied around the waist.

The Japanese clog, or geta, has been worn for centuries in all kinds of weather. It varies in height from two to six inches (5 to 15cm) and varies widely in design.

China

Before China became a republic in 1912, mandarins were high public officials. They wore colorful robes, which had wide, long sleeves and were long, loose, and richly embroidered. Later in the twentieth century, mandarin robes became fashionable with many western women.

Colorful folding fans were first created and used in China.

Chinese men, women, and children often wear dark blue cotton slacks called koo, and a dark blue jacket known as a shan (left). This is considered to be the "everyday workaday dress." Shade straw hats (below) protect field workers from the sun and rain.

Western-style clothing is popular in Asia.

Russian fashion is well-known for its use of fur.

EASTERN EUROPE: RUSSIA

The extremes of winter and summer affected Russian fashion, but no more so than many of the rulers. Russian leaders Peter the Great, Catherine the Great, Alexander I, Nicholas I, and so on, dazzled the world with their extravagance. Their fabulous furs and elaborately decorated fashions reflected the influence of Europe, but with their own style. A traveler to Russia (Theophile Gautier, 1865) once wrote: "Tell me what furs you wear, and I will tell you how much you are worth."

Sarafan

The sarafan (right, figurine on left) is the traditional dress of old Russia and is still worn by Russian peasants. A long, full skirt of brocade or wool is gathered to a sleeveless bodice with either a square or round neckline. This is worn over a full, soft white blouse, which is gathered at the wrists into ruffles or cuffs. An embroidered, sleeveless jacket or bolero is also often worn. Both the overdress and jacket are called sarafans.

A calpac, a traditional cap of Russia

The caftan (right) was a long, coatlike Oriental garment with long sleeves covering the hands. It was held by a cummerbund or hizaam wrapped around the waist. Peter the Great disliked the sleeves, stating to his boyars, "See, these things are in your way. You are safe nowhere with them. At one moment you upset a glass, then you dip them in the sauce."

Caftan

The Cossack officers of World War I (left) wore caftan-like dark coats with flared sleeves. Rows of cartridge pockets were on either side. A black satin muffler and leather belt with sword and dirk, along with leather boots and astrakhan cap completed the outfit. Cossacks are still active in Russia today (above right).

A Russian smock blouse (left, figurine on right) is of heavy white linen with full sleeves, narrow cuffs and a narrow standing collar. The collar, cuffs, and hem are embroidered, as is the left-side opening in front from collar to waist. It is an important garment whether worn with a leather belt or tucked inside the trousers.

Russian peasant women often wear a head-scarf tied under the chin. Because older women refused to discard the headkerchief despite changing fashions, it came to be known as a babushka, *the Russian word for grandmother.*

Russian embroidery is done mostly on linen in brilliantly-colored geometric designs. Embroidery is used on collars, cuffs, and wide hem borders on skirts. Also, this embroidery is worked on holland—a canvas of plain weave, sized and glazed. The canvas is cut away upon completing the embroidery.

WESTERN EUROPE: ENGLAND

Queen Elizabeth (1558 to 1603) popularized the ruff collar, a stiff collar of starched and wired ruffles.

Trade expanded from the years A.D. 1000 to 1500. Marriage between the ruling families of different countries helped spread fashion ideas across Europe. The church insisted that women cover their bodies and hair. However, by the 1300s, the church's rules were ignored as a new rich class of people demanded stylish clothing with jewels and fur.

Cotehardie

A cotehardie, like the one worn by the woman in yellow in the painting at right, is a close-fitting gown with sleeves cut to elbow length and a long trailing cuff called a tippet. Over this was worn a sideless surcoat.

A stomacher (left) is a narrow front panel on a dress that ends in a sharp point. It is worn over a tightly fitting bodice, and usually decorated with lace, ribbons, or jewels. To get into these tightly fitting outfits, some women squeezed into iron corsets (right).

Women's hair

Women wore padded rolls, horned headdresses with veils (right), or braided and coiled their hair in jeweled nets (left).

Liripipe

Starting around the fourteenth century, men covered their heads with a hood and shoulder cape. The hood had a point in the back called a liripipe. The liripipe grew to all lengths over the years, and many ways were devised of draping it about the head. It was either wrapped around the neck and arms, or wrapped around the head like a turban, or sometimes left to simply hang in back. In most cases, the longer hoods were permitted only to nobles, while common people had to wear the shorter liripipes.

A wimple (right) is a white linen head covering, such as the kind worn by nuns.

The points of men's shoes eventually grew to three times the length of the shoe. Some were attached by a light chain to a band at the knee.

Armor

Heavy steel suits of armor were worn by the rich in the twelfth century. To know friend from foe brought about the art of heraldry—symbols and colors depicting one's family history. Gunpowder eventually ended armor's usefulness.

King Henry VIII (1509 to 1547) introduced the style that emphasized his broad shoulders.

SOUTHERN EUROPE: ITALY

Fashions during the Italian Renaissance were known throughout Europe for their daring style.

Italy became the fashion leader during the fifteenth century, or early Renaissance. Italians displayed the body, rather than hiding it. Dresses were low-cut. Buttons allowed for close fitting apparel without belts. Wealthy people wore heavy clothing made of silks, velvets, damasks, or brocades—often embroidered with gold or silver threads or lined with fur.

Gamurra

A gamurra (right), also called a kirtle, was a dress that followed the shape of the body. It was a basic garment, worn with nothing over it for casual indoor use. Gamurras were distinctly soft and loose, with a neckline that was low, round, and wide. They had a separate, short-waisted bodice and a straight, gathered skirt. Sleeves were usually separate from the gown and tied or laced in place. The fabric and color of the sleeves were often different from the gown, with the chemise pulled through the openings between the ties to make little puffs.

The Italian houppelande (left), or cioppa, was shaped like a cone, with narrow shoulders and a full hem. At the high waistline it was pleated into pipelike folds. Sleeves were long, funnel-shaped, and lined with fur or with a contrasting color.

"Slashing" was the practice of slitting materials and pulling the lining through. It was seen in everything from sleeves to shoes. In the image at right, the chemise is pulled through the sleeve openings.

Headdress

A ghirlanda was a woman's headdress made of rich fabric surrounding a padded roll that fit around the crown of the head. It was embroidered with gems and pearls.

A popular hat was the bubble, or turban, which was set back on the head and framed the face.

Doublet

A doublet was a close-fitting jacket that was padded and quilted, and made of velvet, silk, or satin. If a man dared, he wore an extremely short doublet, which became fashionable later in the century.

A common outfit for men during this period included a camise (shirt) and doublet, together with leg hose and a codpiece. The hose was often made of two separate legs with a leather sole attached (no shoes required). The opening at the groin was covered by a codpiece.

There were five main hat styles during this period: turban, roundel, bag hat, sombrero, and fez. The turban (left) was the most popular. Men shaved their heads at the side and back to wear this hat.

NORTHERN EUROPE: FRANCE

Louis XIV in a richly embroidered cassock and matching waistcoat, decorated with large ribbon loops. The hat is an early tricorne.

In the seventeenth century, France became very powerful under the rule of Louis XIV. The French style of dress was rich and elaborate. Out went the stiff, painful clothing of the Renaissance and in came flowing gowns of lace, ribbons, and jewels. The lacy costumes of the Cavaliers and Musketeers became well known. However, French styles contrasted sharply with the plain styles of England's Commonwealth supporters, known as Puritans.

Women's fashion

For the first time since ancient Rome, women showed their arms, as sleeves became elbow length. Beautiful lace sleeve trims adorned the fashions. The stiff ruffs were replaced with large lace collars, worn either high to the neck or fitting around the line of the bodice and fastened with a brooch. The lovely lace was detached for cleaning.

Fontange

Duchesse de Fontanges created a cap with layers of upstanding, pleated, wired ruffles of lawn, lace, and ribbons. It was worn with two long streamers called lappets hanging down the back. The height made it difficult to wear, and it was later shrunk to a smaller lace cap, or commode.

Cavalier

Cavalier-style clothing featured full shirt sleeves gathered into a band at the wrist and trimmed with lace, then turned back over the sleeve of

the doublet. The Musketeers made this style famous. Boots were tight in the leg, wide at the top, and fitted with spurs. Shoe bows and buckles were popular. The baldric (belt) was worn diagonally across the doublet from which swords were hung.

Periwigs and Cassocks

Men wore periwigs, huge cascades of corkscrew curls, rising above the head in two peaks. Underneath, men cut their own hair short or shaved their heads so the wig would fit more snugly. By the late 1600s, men began to tie the wig in a ponytail, which became the fashion of the following century.

The jack boot was a favorite of soldiers and horsemen. It flared widely above the knee.

The cassock ends just above the knees, with sleeves ending at the elbow. Close-set buttons and buttonholes extend all the way down the center front. Over the cassock is a large diagonal sash, which was a status symbol.

Huge bold feather plumes adorned hats (left). Feathers were dyed in the current colors and then curled with a feather curler.

Petticoat breeches (right) were full and gathered in at the knee and decorated with ribbons or lace frills.

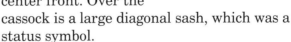

NORTH AMERICA: THE COLONISTS

Pilgrims land at Plymouth Rock, Massachusetts, in 1620.

On December 21, 1620, the Mayflower docked in America. The colonists adopted a plain fashion known as "Puritan Style," which had been worn for nearly a 100 years. The somber dark colors reflected the wearer's disapproval of the morals and politics of the time. Soon more people came to America. Many fashion trends still came from Europe, but the Industrial Revolution transformed the world. New machines wove and knitted cloth. America's independence from Britain came in 1783, and by then Americans were sending cotton cloth to Europe.

Pilgrims

A pilgrim woman typically wore simple dress in plum, gray, or brown. Puffed sleeves were divided into sections. They sometimes carried a fur muff, a soft bag open at each end for warming the hands. An apron was at first worn to protect the dress from stains. Later, it came to be made of fine linen and was part of the fashionable style.

French Americans inspired the simple, light-cotton, Creole-style gown.

Pilgrim men (right) wore a stiff, high-crowned sugarloaf hat that was made of black felt with a ribbon and small buckle. A rabat, or falling band collar, of white lawn was tied with strings. Cuffs were made of the same material. They also typically wore a cloak or hooded cape. A jerkin was a type of man's cotehardie, or shirt. Breeches, or slops, were loose-fitting pants.

Among fashionable colonists of the eighteenth century, a small scarf, or fichu, made of fine lace was worn over low necklines. Until the 1770s, women wore wide dresses, with a shape created by a pannier, or false hips. Hair in the early 1700s was crimped with curling irons and worn in a chignon at the nape of the neck. After 1730, it was swept back from the forehead over pads to an enormous height. Everything was powdered ash blond. A hair creme called pomade kept it all in place. Hairstyles were so high during the 1770s and 1780s that they ran the risk of being set on fire by chandelier candles.

Men's Colonial Fashion

Colonists of the mid-1700s typically wore a tricorne, a three-peaked hat that was worn over powdered hair (either a wig or real hair). Since the powder got on the hat, the tricorne was often carried rather than worn. The jabot was the lace frill worn with a gilet, a vest, or waistcoat. Breeches were knee-length pants fastened with buttons and held up with suspenders made of ribbons. Shoes were black and decorated with buckles. The heels were high and often colored red.

NORTH AMERICA: NATIVE AMERICANS

A Winnebago warrior wore a roach headdress of animal hair if he had killed but not scalped an enemy. An eagle feather was added if a scalp had been taken.

Native Americans' dress varied greatly with the location of their homes. Some Natives Americans of the Plains wore beautifully dyed animal skins and furs, while Northeastern farming tribes used the soft bark of trees and grasses to produce their clothing. Most people associate Native Americans with the elaborate feather headdresses, shields, and clothing they created. The beadwork and embroidery, although quite varied by tribe, is famous, as are the soft deerskin shoes known as moccasins.

European artists John White and Jacques Le Moyne illustrated the Florida Timucua tribe in the 1580s. They wore simple clothing, but adorned their bodies with elaborate tattoos.

Moccasins
Moccasins are a soft leather shoe without a heel. The sole and sides are made of one piece. The edges are joined with a gathered seam to a U-shaped piece, forming the instep. Some moccasins were embroidered with beads and dyed porcupine quills and had a fold-over cuff tied in back.

Apache

Instead of wearing moccasins with separate hide leggings to protect their legs from thornbush, Apaches of the American Southwest wore a one-piece soft boot, or long moccasin, made from antelope skin or deerskin. These boots were often decorated with beadwork or metal studs.

Freezing winters caused northern tribes like the Ojibwa to create winter clothing made of tanned caribou or deer skins with the hair side inward – including coats, mittens, leggings or trousers, moccasins, and hoods. Children sometimes wore winter coats woven from strips of rabbit skin. Decorations varied depending upon the tribe. Easterners painted unique red designs on their coats, while far westerners used porcupine quills, shells, and beads.

Tlingit and Swakiutl

The Tlingit and Swakiutl tribes of the Pacific Northwest are famous for their elaborate costumes and headdresses made for the potlatch ceremony, wherein a person gains wealth and status by giving away gifts. Tlingit women wove dancing dresses from mountain-goat wool and cedar bark.

Inuit

A hooded anorak, or parka, is made of animal skins, such as seal, walrus, or caribou. It traps a layer of insulating air against the body.

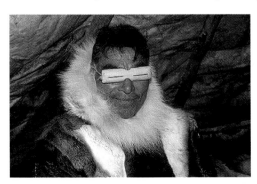

Some Inuit wore waterproof anoraks made from seal intestines. Sunglasses were needed against the blinding glare of snow and ice. Long before Europeans, Arctic people wore wood or bone goggles, blackened on the inside, which blocked most of the sunlight.

NORTH AMERICA: THE 1800s

Trappers wore buckskin tunics with long fringes, which tended to drain off rain.

The push to head West began in the 1800s, and increased with the Gold Rush of 1849. The brave people who loaded their covered wagons with whatever possessions they could bring, soon discovered their travels were filled with hard work, death, and making do. The world around them, however, continued to improve. The power-loom wove huge amounts of cotton cloth, and ready-to-wear clothing had begun to appear in stores.

Pioneer Women
Sunbonnets were made of cotton fabric, fashioned with a brim or poke and held in shape by stitched slots holding thin wooden slats. They were worn to protect the face from the sun and to keep hair in place. In barren areas with little or no brush or trees, women spread their skirts wide to provide privacy for each other to go to the bathroom.

John B. Stetson created the cowboy hat in the 1880s. It was made of straw or felt. A neckerchief or bandana was worn to absorb sweat or tied over the mouth to keep out dust. Vests were common and gave a link to Eastern fashion and a "business" look to the cowboy. Buckskin gloves were worn to protect the hands against rope burns and other hazards. Blue jeans were originally sailing canvas cut and sewn into trousers. Chaperajos, or chaps, protected trousers from brush and thorns. Cowboy boots had two-inch (5 cm) slanted heels to keep the foot in the stirrup.

NORTH AMERICA: CIVIL WAR YEARS

In 1841, Elias Howe patented the sewing machine. Ten years later, Isaac Merrit Singer produced a practical sewing machine and began the concept of mass production of clothing. North Americans continued to follow the fashion trends created by *couturiers* in Europe. During the trying years of the Civil War (1861 to 1865), men wished to look impressive, and followed President Lincoln's formal black suit style. Women followed the rules of *Godey's Lady's Book*, but the layers and layers of underwear gave way to a new invention: the crinoline.

Crinoline

To achieve full skirts, women in the 1840s wore under their dresses: long pantalettes, a chemise, a starched petticoat, a crinoline petticoat, another one that was heavily flounced, and a muslin petticoat. Then came the crinoline (right). Originally, it was a stiff petticoat with a layer of horsehair sandwiched between two layers of cotton. In the 1850s came the cage crinoline. It was dome-shaped and could be made from steel or bamboo hoops. It was difficult to sit down in, and impossible to control in a high wind.

President Abraham Lincoln was known for wearing a tall, silk top hat, also known as a "topper" or "silker." (This picture is of an actor playing Lincoln).

NORTH AMERICA:
TURN OF THE CENTURY

The bustle was a pad worn at the small of the back. The popular hourglass shape was achieved with a tightly cinched corset (opposite) that impaired breathing, eating, walking, even standing!

Women's impractically wide skirts changed to frilled, tiered, gathered-behind skirts in the late 1870s. The crinoline was gone, and in its place were bustles.

In 1876, North Americans were hit by the exercise craze. Bicycling and swimming were popular, forcing designers to provide suitable clothing for women. Shirtwaists and bell skirts helped women in both the business and sporting areas.

But then came the Gibson girl—tall with an s-shaped figure, sweet, graceful, athletic—the image of the new woman. Unfortunately, ordinary females could not fit this image created by New York illustrator Charles Dana Gibson, but for 20 years, they kept trying.

Meanwhile, men's fashions had grown sportier, with blazers and straw hats, although the stiff, high collars, and starched cuffs were still worn for formal occasions.

The cycling craze brought about the split-skirt. Bloomers (right), first introduced by Amelia Bloomer in 1851, were also worn, but often frowned upon.

Women wore bathing dresses (left) with bloomers and stockings, and a corset.

Gibson Girl

A shirtwaist was the woman's version of a man's shirt, and immortalized in the Gibson girl paintings. Leg-o-mutton sleeves were fitted at the forearm, but flared into a balloon shape above the elbow. Bell skirts were shaped with haircloth lining, a cotton material interwoven with horsehair from the tail or mane.

Men's opera hats were made over a collapsible steel frame, allowing the hat to be folded and placed under his seat. Wing collars had pointed turned-back tabs and were worn with a bow tie or ascot. Elastic garters held up men's socks.

Men's bathing suits were of wool. Some were buttoned on the shoulder for ease of dressing.

The straw boater hat was popular during the summer. It was typically worn between June 1 and September 1.

Men's union suits (right) were of knitted cotton or wool, depending on the season.

Knickerbockers (left) were worn while hunting or golfing, and brought about a revival of knee breeches for daywear in the 1880s.

NORTH AMERICA: THE 1910s & 1920s

Raccoon coat

OUR
REGULAR DIVISIONS

Honored and Respected by All

Doughboys went to fight in France in World War I with woolen uniforms and steel helmets.

World War I (1914 to 1918) was known as the Great War because it affected almost every country in the world, causing a rush of young men to join the military. With men off to war, women took over their jobs in the factories, and found they could do the work of a man. Out went painful corsets and in came the straight, comfortable fashions of the Jazz Age. Wealthy young men loved their automobiles, raccoon coats, and Oxford bags. Older men wore fedoras, double-breasted suits, and shoes with spats.

Cloche hats (right) were tight to the head, making short, bobbed hairstyles popular. Bright red lipstick was used to make the cupid-bow mouth. Colored nail varnish was first made at the end of the 1920s.

Flappers

Flappers (left) danced the Charleston wearing fringed, beaded, or sequined fashions. Designer "Coco" Chanel is credited with the flat-chested, dropped-waist dresses of the 1920s.

Boys wore knickerbockers (right), shirts, and sleeveless sweaters with long socks, short boots, and caps. It's a costume that people of today often associate with the boys who sold newspapers.

Gangsters like Leo Lepke (above) liked to wear pin-striped suits during the 1930s.

NORTH AMERICA: THE 1930s

In 1929, the stock market crashed, beginning the Great Depression. Jobs and money were scarce. Americans began making their own clothes from dressmaking patterns first created by Ebenezer Butterick. Movies had a great influence on fashion, and people copied the outfits of their favorite actors. Women began to wear wide-legged pants for sports. Menswear didn't change much from the 1920s. It is often remembered as a time of gangsters with pin-striped suits, shoes with spats, and overcoats.

Bias Cut

The bias cut allowed the dress to cling to the body (left). With these sleek, fitted dresses women no longer had to wear corsets to force their bodies into shape. For the first time, exercise clubs and gyms became popular for women. All well-dressed women wore hats and gloves. Handbags were small. A slim metal box with a chain handle called a minaudier was popular.

Stylish women kept their hair short and waved using permanent-waving products.

Shirley Temple (right) was America's most popular star. Only seven years old in 1935, her smiling face, curls, and talent made her a model for what every parent wanted their little girl to be.

NORTH AMERICA:
THE 1940s

America entered World War II in December, 1941. There became a worldwide shortage of fabrics, and many fashion industry workers were transferred to war-related industries. In 1942, victory suits, clothes designed to last and to use fabric and trimmings in an economical way, were introduced. Many men and women were in the armed forces, and those uniforms influenced clothing on the homefront.

The fictional Rosie the Riveter showed a strong woman able to build war machines. Women across the country began wearing pants (right).

Victory Suit
A victory suit (left) of long-wearing tweed, with square, padded shoulders was fashioned after military uniforms. Women wore sensible shoes with a wedge-sole.

On July 5, 1946, Micheline Bernardini (right) wore the bikini swimsuit, named after Bikini Atoll in the Pacific. People were shocked to think women would appear in public in something that fit into a matchbox.

Silk was rare and sheer, hard-wearing cheap nylon stockings became popular. However, if neither could be had, women wore leg makeup—even drawing a "seam" up the back of their legs to look as though they were wearing stockings (left).

NORTH AMERICA: THE 1950s

After the war, designer Christian Dior introduced the "New Look" for women with romantic clothes made with lots of material. Suits were standard for men, but casual clothes, such as sports jackets and cardigans, became popular. What was really new was fashion for teenagers. Children had always worn clothes similar to adults. However, the 1950s changed that, as young people began wearing the fashions of their favorite movie stars.

A teenager in a poodle skirt and white blouse. Pencil skirts and casual sweaters were also popular.

The "New Look"
The "New Look" by Christian Dior (left) featured full skirts that used as much as 18 yards (16 m) of material.

Once again, women wore corsets and girdles to achieve the desired narrow waist (above).

Blue jeans and leather jackets were once workwear, but during the 1950s they became the standard teen "uniform."

Men's Clothing
Men still went to work in suits—now with very narrow ties (left)—but they came home to change into comfortable sweaters or cardigans.

Pompadour hairstyles (left) were formed with lots of hair gel.

NORTH AMERICA: THE 1960s & 1970s

Hippies started a counterculture fashion trend during the 1960s.

Fashions took wild turns in the 1960s as designers brought out everything from paper to plastic clothing. The youth market drove the industry, with bell-bottom trousers, beads, vests, and psychedelic patterns. Many adults complained they couldn't tell boys from girls as hippies filled college campuses. Meanwhile, women were faced with all lengths of skirt. The 1970s brought the disco look, with platform shoes, dresses with side slits, and the leisure suit.

Pillbox Hat
Jackie Kennedy, wife of President John F. Kennedy, popularized the pillbox hat, which was a small, round hat made of stiffened fabric worn on the back of the head.

Women could choose between the maxi-, midi-, and miniskirts of the 1960s. Knee-length boots were often worn with miniskirts.

Hippies often wore granny glasses, tie-dyed or flowered shirts, vests, love beads, and bell-bottoms. Peace symbols were everywhere as the war in Vietnam raged.

Disco

The 1970s was the disco era. Disco became a way of life, not just a type of music. Men wore bell-bottoms, but the fabric was polyester, acrylic, and lycra.

Women wore ruffled and loose dresses, usually stopping at the knee. Platform shoes with skyscraper heels (above, left) went extreme in the 1970s, sometimes featuring such things as live goldfish in the heels!

African Americans turned to a natural Afro hairstyle.

Hip huggers (left) and hot pants (above) were worn in the early 1970s, sometimes even by men. Colors were loud and clashing.

Bell-bottom jeans flared very wide in the '70s. Patchwork denim men's shirts were also very fashionable, especially when unbuttoned and worn with gold chains around the neck.

The leisure suit led a short life in the late 1970s.

Punk rocker

In the 1980s, people rejected the disco look of the previous decade, but they continued to be influenced by the fashions of their favorite movie stars and singers. Punk rockers turned up with wildly colored, spiked hairstyles, slashed jeans, and body piercings. Designer jeans and shirts became popular.

In the 1950s, people expected to see rocket ships and spacewear with the dawn of the millennium. Those creative imaginations were disappointed, however, as blue jeans and T-shirts continue to be the standard wear.

More and more women entered the corporate boardroom during the '80s. Women's business suits used shoulder pads, resembling those of the '30s, but with brighter colors.

New Wave bands (like the Boomtown Rats, right) had a distinct influence on fashion. Gone was the disco look. In its place were wild hairstyles, bright colors, suit coats, and skinny ties, especially leather.

Another fashion fad started in the '80s with the exercise boom (left). Exercise clothes became bright and worn casually. Lycra and spandex were common materials, often in brilliant colors.

Punk rockers used sticky hair gel to achieve their spikes.

Designer Clothes

Starting in the '80s, but really taking off in the '90s, clothing designers put their names on jeans, T-shirts, tennis shoes, and even swimsuits. To stay fashionable, today's teenagers find it extremely important to wear some article of clothing that has a designer label on it, like Calvin Klein, Tommy Hilfiger, or Ralph Lauren.

For women's fashion, the '90s is a mixture of many different styles from several eras. This dress (left), like much fashion of the '90s, is inspired by dresses of the '20s and '30s.

Blue jeans may change from narrow legs to wide legs, may be slashed, stonewashed, black, purple, or blue, but this is one clothing article that appears to be here to stay.

CLOTHING

Soldiers wear armor in England

| 1000 | 1050 | 1100 | 1150 | 1200 |

Italians create close-fitting clothes

King Henry VIII introduces style with broad shoulders

Queen Elizabeth popularizes the ruff in England

| 1400 | 1450 | 1500 | 1550 | 1600 |

Power-looms weave large amounts of cotton cloth; ready-to-wear clothing appears in stores

Elias Howe patents sewing machine (1841); women wear full skirts and crinoline

| 1800 | 1810 | 1820 | 1830 | 1840 | 1850 |

Mandarin robes become fashionable in the West

Coco Chanel creates drop-waist dresses; nail varnish first made

Men's pin-striped suits become popular

American women start to wear pants; victory suits introduced in America (1942); Micheline Bernardini wears first bikini bathing suit (1946)

| 1900 | 1910 | 1920 | 1930 | 1940 | 1950 |

MILESTONES

English men cover their heads with a hood and shoulder cape

1200	1250	1300	1350	1400

Pilgrims wear Puritan style (1620s)

Men tie their wigs into ponytails

Tricorne hats worn, women use curling irons, wear chignons, use pomade to sweep hair from their faces, wear wide dresses with false hips; hairstyles gain great height (1730)

Fashionable colonists wear small scarves; American colonists exporting cotton cloth to Europe (1783)

1600	1650	1700	1750	1800

Cage crinoline appears; Singer produces first practical sewing machine, Amelia Bloomer introduces bloomers for women (1851)

Women wear gathered-behind skirts; exercise craze creates new practical clothing for women (1876)

John B. Stetson creates the Stetson hat; knee breeches regain popularity

1850	1860	1870	1880	1890	1900

Poodle skirts, pencil skirts, leather jackets, and blue jeans are popular among teens; women wear Dior's "New Look"

Mini-skirts worn with knee-length boots; pillbox hat gains popularity

Bell-bottoms, hip huggers, Afros, and leisure suits gain popularity

Spandex used in exercise clothing; designer-name clothes gain popularity

1950	1960	1970	1980	1990	2000

43

GLOSSARY

acrylic - a quick-drying man-made textile fiber.

alpaca - a domesticated mammal from Peru. Wool from the alpaca is woven into a thin cloth.

alum - a chemical made from potassium aluminum sulfate or ammonium aluminum sulfate that constricts and binds together soft organic tissue.

anklets - an ornament worn around the ankles.

armlets - a band of cloth or metal worn around the arm.

ascot - a wide neck scarf that is looped under the chin.

astrakhan - a wool cloth with a curled and looped pile.

beadwork - ornamental work done with beads.

bell-bottoms - pants that gradually flare below the knee and resemble the shape of a bell.

bell skirt - a skirt that is narrow at the waist and flared at the hem, resembling a bell.

bias cut - a line that is cut diagonally to the edge of fabric.

blazer - a sportcoat with a notched collar and patch pockets.

bloomers - baggy, loose pants gathered at the knee for use by women in sports.

bodice - the upper part of a woman's dress.

boyar - a member of the Russian aristocracy below the rank of ruling prince.

breeches - short, snug-fitting pants worn at or just below the knee.

caftan - an ankle-length garment with long sleeves, usually made of cotton or silk.

camise - a light, loose, long-sleeved shirt, gown, or tunic.

cardigan - a sweater or jacket that opens all the way in front and usually does not have a collar.

cascade - a series of small waterfalls, or something that resembles this.

cassock - a loose, ankle-length garment.

cavalier - an armed horseman.

chemise - a woman's one-piece undergarment.

climate - the average weather conditions of a place or region.

codpiece - a flap that hides the opening in the front of a pair of breeches.

corkscrew - a long, spiral shape.

corset - a close-fitting support undergarment that is laced tightly and extends form the chest to below the hips.

counter culture - acting against the accepted culture of a society.

courtier - a person associated with a royal court.

cummerbund - a broad waistband usually worn in place of a vest with men's dress clothes.

cut-pile cloth - cloth with a raised surface made of fabric loops that have the tops cut off.

damask - fabric such as linen, cotton, or silk with flat patterns woven in satin on a plain woven background.

deform - to spoil the shape of something.

dirk - a long, straight-sided dagger.

double-breasted - a garment type where one half of the front overlaps the other half, with two rows of buttons and one row of buttonholes.

doublet - a close-fitting waist-length jacket with or without sleeves.

elaborate - complex in detail.

embroidery - decorative designs made by needlework.

envelop - to enclose or enfold completely.

family crest - an emblem that identifies a family.

feminine - characteristic of or appropriate for a woman.

fez - a brimless, cone-shaped hat that is flat on top.

filament - a single thread or a thin, flexible threadlike object.

fillet - a ribbon or narrow strip of cloth used as a headband.

flounce - a wide, ornamental ruffle.

frill - a gathered, cut, or bias-cut fabric edging used on clothing.

garter - a band worn to hold up a stocking or sock.

geometric - using straight or curving lines in design.

granny glasses - glasses with wire frames and round, oval, or square lenses.

groin - the juncture of the lower abdomen and inner thigh.

headband - a strip of cloth worn around the head.

headdress - a covering for the head.

hippie - a person who rejects the culture of an established society.

instep - the arched middle portion of the human foot.

insulate - to separate from a conductor of heat, electricity, or sound.

intestine - the tube-shaped canal that extends from the stomach to the anus.

jodhpur - riding pants that are cut full at the hip and close-fitting from the knee to the ankle.

knickerbockers - loose-fitting short pants gathered at the knee.

lawn - a lightweight, sheer cotton fabric used for blouses and handkerchiefs.

leg-o-mutton sleeve - shaped like the leg of a mutton. It is usually much bigger around one end than the other.

leggings - coverings of cloth or leather that are worn on the legs.

lip plug - usually a ring-shaped object that is inserted into the lip for decoration. It is used by primitive societies.

llama - a South American animal with a thick, woolly coat.

Lycra - a trademarked name for a fabric with spandex in it.

maguey cactus - a Mexican plant that yields long, tough fibers.

mandarin - a high official of China under the empire.

masculine - characteristic of or appropriate for a man.

Mesoamerica - the areas in the central part of the Americas that were highly civilized before Columbus arrived.

mollusk - any of a group of animals without backbones. They usually have soft bodies protected by a shell, such as a clam or oyster.

muffler - a scarf worn around the neck.

musketeer - a soldier armed with a musket.

muslin - a plain-woven sheer to coarse cotton fabric.

nail varnish - a colored liquid applied to fingernails that is usually worn only by women. When it dries, it has a smooth, glossy appearance.

neckerchief - a scarf of kerchief worn around the neck.

overdress - a dress worn over another.

pantalets - long, ruffled drawers formerly worn by women and girls.

pantaloon - tight-fitting trousers that usually have straps passing under the instep. These pants were usually worn by men.

pencil skirt - a long, close-fitting, straight skirt.

petticoat - a skirt or slip worn as an undergarment.

pile - the raised cut or uncut loops of yarn that form the surface of a fabric.

pinstripe - a very thin stripe that is usually on a fabric.

polyester - a light, man-made resin that is used to make fiber. The fiber is then woven into fabric.

pomade - a perfumed ointment used to style hair.

pompadour - a hairstyle for men and women. Men style their hair into a high mound in front. Women style their hair into a loose, full roll around the face.

potlatch - a ceremonial feast of Native Americans of the northwest coast.

psychedelic - of, characterized by, or causing hallucinations or a state like a trance.

quetzal - a Central American bird with shiny green and bright red feathers. The male has a long tail.

raffia - a strong fiber from the leaves of a palm tree.

Renaissance - a revival of art and literature that began in Italy in the fourteenth century.

ruff - a stiff, circular frill worn as a collar by men and women in the fifteenth, sixteenth, and seventeenth centuries.

sheik - an Arab chief.

shirtwaist - a woman's tailored garment with details copied from men's shirts.

Sikh - a follower of a religion developed in about A.D. 1500 that combines elements of Hinduism and Islam.

skullcap - a close-fitting cap without a brim.

smock - a loose outergarment, usually worn to protect clothing.

sombrero - a hat with a broad brim, worn especially in Mexico and the southwestern United States.

spandex - an elastic-like fabric.

spats - a cloth or leather covering worn over the instep of a shoe.

status - a person's position or rank.

stencil - a thin sheet, usually of metal or paper, with a cutout pattern. The sheet is put onto another surface to be decorated. Only the areas that show through the cutouts are painted or inked.

stirrup - one of a pair of metal, wooden, or leather loops or rings, flattened on the bottom and suspended from a saddle. They support a rider's foot in mounting and riding.

stylized - to make something following the rules of a specific style.

surcoat - an outer coat. It was usually a short garment worn over armor during the Middle Ages.

suspender - straps used to hold up pants or a skirt. The straps are attached at the garment's waistband and go over the shoulders.

tarboosh - a red hat similar to the fez.

tattoo - a permanent mark made on the skin. Tattoos are usually designs or figures.

tendons - a strong cord or band of tissue that attaches a muscle to a bone or other part of the body.

tier - a series of layers.

tweed - a rough fabric made of wool. It is woven with yarns of two or more colors.

union suit - an undergarment with the shirt and drawers in one piece.

velvet - a fabric made of silk, rayon, nylon, or other fabric. It has a thick, smooth pile.

vicuña - a South American animal related to the llama. Vicuñas have silky, wool coats.

waistcoat - an ornamental garment worn under a doublet.

yucca - a plant in the southwestern United States and Latin America. It has a woody stem and bears white clusters of bell-shaped flowers.

INTERNET SITES

The Museum of Costume
http://www.museumofcostume.co.uk/
The Museum of Costume, in England, contains a wealth of information and pictures of fashion dating from medieval times to today. The museum also includes a wide array of knitting and dressmaking patterns, fashion plates, and fashion reports from current newspapers and magazines.

The Bad Fads Museum
www.badfads.com/fashionframe.html
This site displays fads you wished would stay forever or wish would never come back, like leisure suits, Afro haircuts, and nehru jackets.

Fashion Through the Decades
http://drake.marin.k12.ca.us/students/gallaghj/fashion/
fash_thru_decade.html
This site provides an entertaining look at fashion of the twentieth century from the 1920s to the 1990s.

These sites are subject to change. Go to your favorite search engine and try "clothing" for more sites.

FOR FURTHER READING

Knight, Margaret and Penny Ives. *Fashion through the Ages*. New York: Viking Penguin, 1998.

Paul, Penelope. *Costume and Clothes*. New York: Thomson Learning, 1995.

Rowland-Warne, L. and Liz Maaulay. *Costume*. New York: Alfred A. Knopf, 1992.

Ventura, Piero and Max Casalini. *Clothing: Garments, Styles, and Uses*. New York: Houghton Mifflin Company, 1993.

INDEX